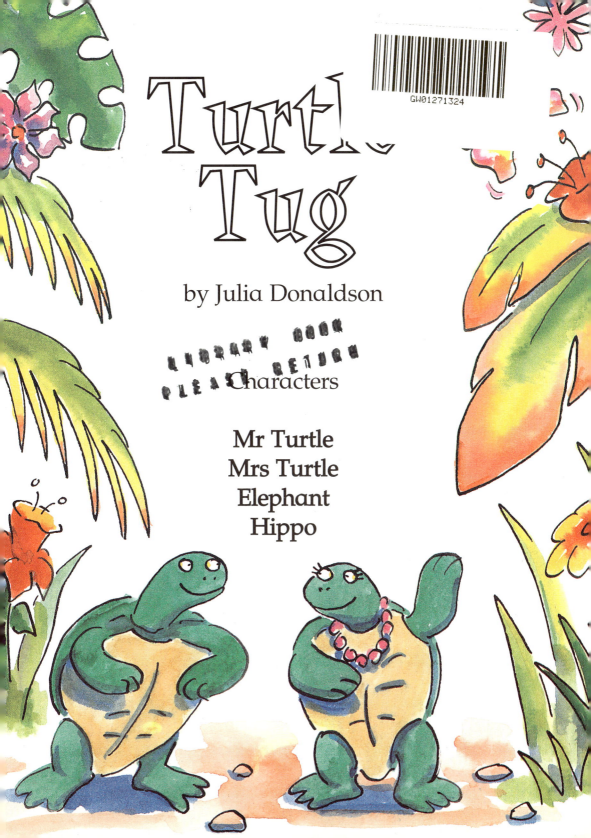

Turtle Tug

by Julia Donaldson

Characters

Mr Turtle
Mrs Turtle
Elephant
Hippo

*Elephant lives on one bank of a river.
Hippo lives on the other bank.
The two turtles live on a little island in the middle of the river.*

Scene 1

(Mr Turtle swims over to Elephant's bank.)

Mr Turtle: Hello Elephant.

Elephant: It's *Sir* Elephant.

Mr Turtle: All right then, *Sir* Elephant. It's Mrs Turtle's birthday tomorrow. Can you come to her party?

Elephant: Don't be silly, Turtle.

Mr Turtle: I'm not being silly. Mouse can come and Monkey can come. Why can't you?

Elephant: Me? A big strong elephant like me, come to a little turtle's party? No thank you.

Mr Turtle: All right, Elephant, but you'll miss all the fun.

Elephant: It's *Sir* Elephant, and it's no fun for me to mix with weak little animals like you.

Mr Turtle: If you say so, *Sir* Elephant.

Scene 2

(Mrs Turtle swims over to Hippo's bank of the river.)

Mrs Turtle: Hello, Hippo.

Hippo: Call me *Madam* Hippo.

Mrs Turtle: All right then, *Madam* Hippo. It's my birthday tomorrow. Can you come to my party?

Hippo: Don't be silly.

Mrs Turtle: I'm not being silly. Goat can come and Rabbit can come. Why can't you?

Hippo: Me? A big strong hippo like me, come to a little turtle's party? No thank you.

Mrs Turtle: All right, Hippo, but you'll miss all the fun.

Hippo: It's *Madam* Hippo, and it's no fun for me to mix with weak little animals like you.

Mrs Turtle: If you say so, *Madam* Hippo.

Scene 3

(Mr and Mrs Turtle are at home on Turtle Island.)

Mrs Turtle: How did you get on?

Mr Turtle: Mouse can come and Monkey can come, but not Elephant.

Mrs Turtle: Why not?

Mr Turtle: He says he's too big and strong.

Mrs Turtle: He's so snooty!

Mr Turtle: How did *you* get on?

Mrs Turtle: Goat can come and Rabbit can come, but not Hippo.

Mr Turtle: Why not?

Mrs Turtle: She says she's too big and strong.

Mr Turtle: Just like Elephant. How can we stop the two of them being so snooty?

Mrs Turtle: Let me think. Do we have a long rope?

Mr Turtle: Yes.

Mrs Turtle: And a sharp stone?

Mr Turtle: I can find one.

Mrs Turtle: Good. Then I think there is a way!

Scene 4

(Mr Turtle swims over to Elephant's bank of the river.)

Mr Turtle: Hello, Elephant.

Elephant: It's *Sir* Elephant! What is it?

Mr Turtle: I'd like to have a tug-of-war with you.

Elephant: Me? Big strong Elephant, have a tug-of-war with a weak little turtle?

Mr Turtle: I'm just as strong as you!

Elephant: Ha ha! All right, we'll try it.

Mr Turtle: Good. Take this end of the rope and when I shout "go," you pull.

(Mr Turtle swims back across the river and meets Mrs Turtle on Turtle Island. He gives her the other end of the rope.)

Mr Turtle: Here's the end of the rope.

Mrs Turtle: Thank you.

(Mrs Turtle swims to Hippo's bank of the river.)

Mrs Turtle: Hello, Hippo!

Hippo: It's *Madam* Hippo. What do you want now?

Mrs Turtle: I'd like to have a tug-of-war with you.

Hippo: Me? Big strong Hippo have a tug-of-war with a weak little turtle?

Mrs Turtle: I may be little but I'm not weak.

Hippo: Ha ha! All right, we'll try it.

Mrs Turtle: Take this end of the rope and when I shout "go," you pull.

(Mrs Turtle swims back to Mr Turtle on Turtle Island.)

Mr Turtle: All right?

Mrs Turtle: Yes.

Mr Turtle: Let's shout then.

Mr and Mrs Turtle: GO!

(Elephant and Hippo both pull the rope.)

Elephant: Turtle isn't all that weak.

Hippo: I didn't think Mrs Turtle was so strong!

Elephant: I'll have to pull harder.

Hippo: If I don't pull harder she'll pull me into the river!

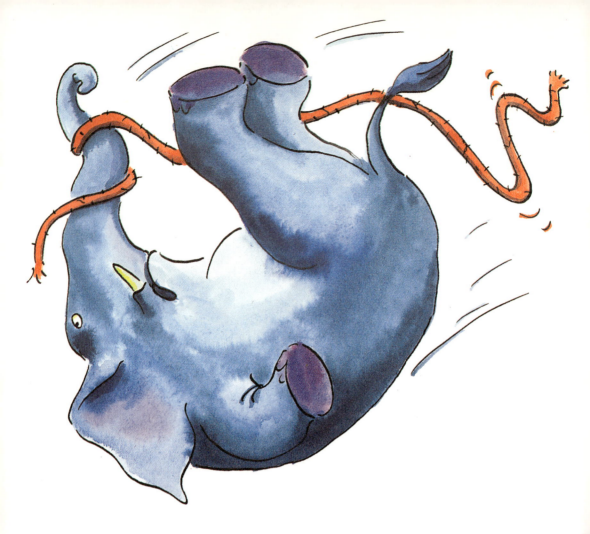

Mrs Turtle: Have you got the sharp stone?

Mr Turtle: Here it is.

Mrs Turtle: Good. Then cut the rope.

(Mr Turtle cuts the rope, and Elephant and Hippo both fall over backwards. Mr Turtle swims to Elephant's bank.)

Mr Turtle: Hello, Sir Elephant. Are you all right?

Elephant: You don't have to call me *Sir* Elephant. Yes, thank you, but I got a surprise. You *are* strong, just as strong as me!

Mr Turtle: I said so, didn't I?

Elephant: Yes you did. I'm sorry I was so snooty.

Mr Turtle: That's all right, Elephant. See you at the party!

(Mrs Turtle swims to Hippo's bank.)

Mrs Turtle: Can I help you up, Madam Hippo?

Hippo: Thank you – and you don't have to call me *Madam*. I didn't think you were so strong. I'm sorry I was so snooty.

Mrs Turtle: That's all right, Hippo. By the way, are you coming to my party?

Hippo: Yes please. And what do you want for your birthday?

Mrs Turtle: How about a new rope!